How To Teach

Butterfly

Basic technique drills, step-by-step lesson plans and everything in-between

A swimming teacher's definitive guide to teaching butterfly swimming stroke

Mark Young

A Catalogue record for this book is available from the British Library

ISBN 9780995484252

Published by: Educate & Learn Publishing, Hertfordshire, UK

Graphics by Mark Young, courtesy of Poser V6.0

Design and typeset by Mark Young

Published in association with www.swim-teach.com

Note: This book is intended for guidance and support only. The material contained here should accompany additional course material set on an official swimming teaching course by an official Swimming Association. Neither the author nor the publisher can accept responsibility for any injury or loss sustained as a result of the use of this material.

Author Online!
For more resources and swimming help visit
Mark Young's website at

www.swim-teach.com

Teaching · Learning · Achieving · Professional Swimming Help Online

Mark Young is a well-established swimming instructor with decades of experience of teaching thousands of adults and children to swim. He has taken nervous, frightened children and adults with a fear of water and made them happy and confident swimmers. He has also turned many of average ability into advanced swimmers. This book draws on his experiences and countless successes to put together this simplistic methodical approach to teaching swimming.

Also by Mark Young

Teaching Guides
How To Be A Swimming Teacher
101 Swimming Lesson Plans
How To Teach Front Crawl
How To Teach Breaststroke
How To Teach Backstroke

Learn to Swim Guides
The Complete Beginners Guide to Swimming
How To Swim Front Crawl
How To Swim Breaststroke
How To Swim Backstroke
How To Swim Butterfly
The Swimming Strokes Book

Contents

Introduction

Butterfly swimming stroke is both powerful and elegant when swum correctly. It requires strong core muscles, upper body strength, and shoulder flexibility. Get the undulating body movement in sync with the arm pulls, breathing and leg kicks, and your pupils will be on the road to mastering this most spectacular of the four basic strokes.

What Makes A Good Teacher?

'A teacher is one who makes himself progressively unnecessary.'
Thomas Carruthers

What makes a good teacher?

A teacher is looked up to by their pupils as a role model and a source of knowledge and guidance. A teacher possesses several key characteristics that make him or her individual and it is these personal characteristics that can determine a teacher's level of success.

A good swimming teacher requires a wide range of qualities. You will probably be stronger in some areas than others and as you gain experience you will build your competence in all areas.

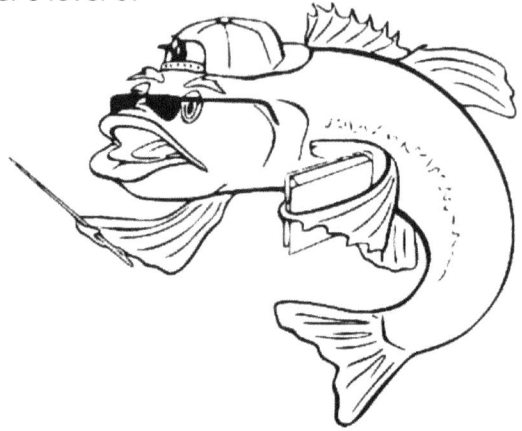

Teaching Qualities

To be a good teacher and role model to your pupils, you need to possess some essential qualities. These are:

Knowledge
Having sound knowledge of your subject gains you respect, not only from your pupils but from parents and other swimming teachers. You will need to keep your knowledge up to date and always admit when you don't know the answer, but make it your business to find out.

Empathy
Teaching swimming requires empathy on all levels. For example, the child who is scared and has every reason to be, the adult who is equally scared or even embarrassed, the child who is over-excited at the prospect of going in the pool and the child who is trying hard but not keeping up with the rest.

Patience

All of the above examples that require empathy will also test your patience. As a teacher, you have to accept that not everybody learns at the same rate. Children's behaviour and attention spans will also try your patience at times. Whatever is thrown at you, you must show patience and control at all times.

Control and Management

It goes without saying that you must have control over your class, especially with children in a pool. In the classroom at school, children know what is expected of them but this is not always the case in the swimming pool. Children have to be controlled for safety purposes as well as learning purposes.

If pupils are being unruly throughout the lesson then not only is the lesson unsafe, but they are not learning anything. The golden rule is to set out your stall early on to show them who is boss. That is not to say that you have to 'rule with fear', otherwise pupils will not want to have swimming lessons with you, just let those that step out of line know they have done so and that it will not be tolerated.

Effective Communication

As a teacher, your job is to pass on information effectively and clearly, and your ability to do this will determine how quickly your pupils learn. Knowledge of your subject is also essential, but how you convey that knowledge is far more important. You could be a world expert on the human body and the scientific principles behind swimming but if you are not able to pass that expertise onto eager-to- learn pupils clearly and concisely, then you are not a good teacher!

Basic Principles of Effective Communication

Positioning

Where you position yourself on the poolside will determine how well your pupils can see and hear you. Study the pool diagrams in the planning and organisation section for best practice.

Clarity

Passing information on clearly will ensure your pupils do exactly what you want them to.

Conciseness

Keep your teaching concise to avoid your pupils becoming confused or taking in the wrong pieces of information.

Accuracy

Your teaching has to be accurate as you will be copied, mimicked and quoted especially by children. Inaccuracy will result in your pupils not learning and in you gaining a reputation as a poor teacher.

Enthusiasm

A sure way to motivate your class and get results is to have an enthusiastic approach. Enthusiasm is infectious and if you are full of it when you teach, your pupils will put every effort into what you ask them to do.

Interest

If the content of what you teach is not interesting then your pupils will not listen and become distracted. Enthusiasm and interesting content go hand in hand, as one breeds the other. The most uninteresting subject can be made interesting with an injection of enthusiasm.

Appropriateness

The teaching points and practices you use will determine the success and outcome of the lesson. If your methods are not appropriate, the pupils do not learn and the lesson becomes pointless.

Two-way

Communication works both ways. Ask your pupils questions and listen carefully to those who answer and how they answer. Encourage them to ask you questions at appropriate times.

Motivation

As a teacher, you are also a motivator. Some pupils you teach will need more motivation than others. Most children can't wait to get into the pool and start swimming and impress the teacher.

You will, however, come across children who have swimming lessons because they have been made to do so by their parents, whether they need them or not. Either way, a motivating teacher brings out the best in pupils.

Praise

This is the easiest, most common form of motivation. Remember to praise effort as well as success.

Feedback

This is a more detailed, constructive form of praise. The pupils are given a clearer picture of how they are performing and improving. If feedback is to be motivational it has to be positive.

For example, a swimmer returns to the poolside after practising butterfly leg kick unsuccessfully. Your job is to teach and motivate them. Your feedback should go something like this:

'Well done, that was a good try' (praise for the effort)
'You were kicking with your legs together, which is good, well done.' (positive feedback)
'Try again, and this time bend your knees so that you can kick with more power.' (feedback in the form of a teaching point)
Avoid negative feedback, for example, *'Don't kick your legs straight.'*

Teaching Adults

Adults will arrive on the poolside in all shapes and sizes and with differing levels of confidence. One thing that they will all have in common, however, is that they will all appreciate a relaxed and informal approach to being taught to swim.

Butterfly stroke is considered an advanced swimming stroke, so adults who want to swim it are unlikely to be complete beginners. They are likely to have some swimming experience and be confident in the water. If a total beginner does want to learn butterfly before any other stroke, it would be wise to teach them the basics of breaststroke first to help get them used to the simultaneous movements of the arms and legs. It will also prepare them for the basics of floating, gliding and breathing. Teaching adults, even confident ones, how to swim butterfly still brings some barriers and limitations. These include:

Lack of Flexibility

Generally speaking, adults lack flexibility all over, so when it comes to swimming butterfly the main areas that require large degrees of movement are the shoulders and hips. As a result, their arm action and body undulation can often be quite limited. Arm recovery over the water is often shortened, and hand and arm entry can lack a stretch forward.

Another area that adults often lack flexibility is in their ankles. This can affect the leg kick by preventing the feet and toes from pointing as they kick, which can make the overall kick inefficient and cause drag. A lack of movement in the ankles also means losing the relaxed flipper-like action as they kick.

This lack of flexibility often makes for a very inefficient swimming stroke.

Lack of Fitness

Whilst a lack of general fitness and stamina is not always the case for adults in the swimming pool, learning to swim butterfly could be a relatively new challenge, so it is fair to say they lack 'swimming fitness'. The explosive nature of butterfly and the sheer power needed from the kicks, arm-pulls, and breathing can place enormous demands on the cardiovascular system, resulting in adults becoming very tired very quickly. This is very common.

Add together these two most common limitations and you have what most swimming teachers experience when teaching adults to swim - very slow progress.

Slow progress in adults learning to swim is completely normal and should not be looked upon negatively.

As a swimming teacher, you can do a few things to help.

- Be calm, relaxed and informal in your teaching style as this will help relax your adult and keep them at ease.
- Adjust your expectations accordingly.
- Take their limitations into account when planning. Exercises and drills that suit one swimmer may not work for another.
- Be flexible in your approach. For example, fins or hand paddles (usually used in advanced drills) can often benefit adult beginners, as long as they do not become reliant on them.
- Be sensitive to their frustrations and always show empathy and be supportive in your response.
- Above all, use plenty of praise to stimulate and maintain motivation. At the end of each lesson, pick out the parts they showed progress in and highlight them as achievements of the session, however small they may be.

Equipment

Equipment

Floats and kickboards

When used correctly swimming floats can help develop specific parts of your technique. They are suitable for non-swimmers right up to advanced swimmers and can be used by both adults and children.

Swim floats are used by swimming teachers as part of lessons for many different exercises. They can be used by non-swimmers to strengthen and by established swimmers to isolate and perfect technique.

For example, the weak non-swimmer can use two floats, one placed under each arm, to help strengthen their leg kick. The floats will provide stability and help boost confidence, whilst encouraging a fast and confident leg kick.

Advantages:
- Very versatile and can help enhance a wide range of butterfly drills.
- Can be used in addition to other aids.
- Can be used in place of other types of swimming aid to encourage progression and enhance strength and stamina.
- When used individually floats can help gain leg or arm strength.
- Fine-tune technique by encouraging a swimmer to focus on a certain area of their swimming stroke.
- Cheap to buy and easy to store. Also easy to use with large groups.

Disadvantages:

- Usually not suitable for very young children or babies but this is less relevant as they would not usually be learning butterfly stroke.
- Require close supervision if using with beginner children

Common Mistakes to Watch Out For

It's difficult to use a float incorrectly because they are such a simple piece of swimming equipment. However, there are a couple of points to watch out for when using floats to teach children.

Firstly, it is common for children to grip the float too tightly, especially if they are a nervous beginner. They squeeze the float in their hand, resulting in a very tired hand grip and the focus away from the part of their swimming they are supposed to be concentrating on.

Secondly, it is common for children to bare their weight onto the float, causing it to submerge. Once again this is easily done by the nervous beginner as they attempt to climb above the water surface instead of laying on the surface. Reassuring them and helping them to relax by advising them to "let the float support you", will go some way to helping children to get the most out of swimming floats.

These common problems can take time to fix as the swimmer begins to learn how to relax and become comfortable in the water. As long as the teacher is aware and the swimmer is made aware, then gradual progress can be made.

Woggle or Noodle

One of the most popular buoyancy aids, the swimming noodle, is a simple polythene foam cylinder. One of the most popular and widely used floats during swimming lessons.

Sometimes called a 'woggle', it is cheap to make, cheap to buy and easy to use in large group swimming lessons.

The main advantage is that it provides a high level of support whilst at the same time allowing the swimmer movement of their arms and legs. The swimmer can learn and experience propulsion through the water from both the arms and the legs.

The noodle is very versatile and as it is not a fixed aid, it can be used and removed with ease. It can also add a sense of fun to swimming as it can be tucked under the arms on the front and the back as well as placed between the legs and used as a 'horse'. The noodle has some uses when teaching butterfly technique but they are limited.

Advantages and Disadvantages of a Swimming Noodle

Advantages:

- Provides a high level of support for children of all sizes.
- Gives a sense of independence in the water with the minimum of support.
- Allows freedom of movement.
- Boosts confidence in the nervous beginner.
- Able to support adult beginners
- Easy to fit and remove, so ideal for use in group swimming lessons.
- Allows freedom of movement.

Disadvantages:

- Limited or no use for advanced swimmers.
- Nervous swimmers can 'clamp' it between their body and their arms, restricting their arm action.
- Can cause very buoyant swimmers to tip forwards.

Pull Buoy

A pull buoy is a figure-eight shaped piece of solid foam and used mainly by established and advanced swimmers.

It is placed between the legs in the upper thigh area to provide support to the body so the swimmer can swim without kicking the legs. This allows them to focus on other parts of their swimming stroke, such as arm technique or breathing technique.

This type of swimming aid is most useful when learning and practising front crawl and butterfly techniques.

These training aids are most commonly used by competitive swimmers during their training sessions. They are designed to restrict the use of the swimmer's lower body, causing a greater intensity on the arms and upper body.

The nature of holding it between the legs by squeezing the thighs together also helps to keep the lower body in a streamlined and efficient shape during the swim. By isolating the upper body, the swimmer can focus completely on their arm or breathing technique, whilst the float assists to keep the lower body afloat.

They also help to strengthen the upper body and core muscles by eliminating the kick propulsion, while helping to keep the body position correct in the water.

This type of swimming aid is available in a smaller size for younger swimmers as well as full size for adults.

Pull Buoy Advantages and Disadvantages

Advantages:

- Provide good isolation of the upper body whilst keeping the lower body buoyant.

- Ideal for work-outs and training and therefore more suited to established and advanced swimmers.
- Increased core strength
- Available in adult and junior sizes

Disadvantages:

- Not suitable for non-swimmers and beginners.
- Can place stress on the lower back when used for butterfly drills, so they must be used with caution.

Sinkers

Sinkers are objects such as sticks, hoops and toys that sink to the bottom of the pool. They are a great way to teach children breath control by encouraging them to submerge.

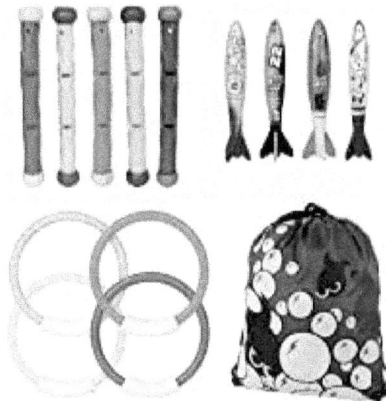

Sinkers can be used in both shallow and deep water and vary in design to cater for a range of ages. Although their uses rarely target a specific swimming stroke, they can open up a huge range of contrasting and complementary activities.

To children, sinkers are the equivalent of toys, so a swimming teacher with a creative imagination can use them to spark excitement and get some fantastic results.

Hand Paddles

Hand paddles develop power in the arms, chest, shoulders and back muscles. They come in the form of large plastic paddles that strap to the palms of the hands and prevent the water from passing through the fingers.

The swimmer can use hand paddles to enhance their feel for the water, which will help to improve their technique.

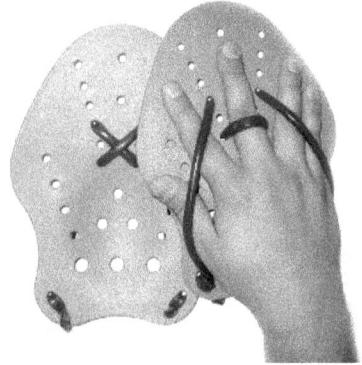

Butterfly Technique

Butterfly

Butterfly stroke is the most recent stroke, developed in the 1930s, and it is the second-fastest stroke to Front Crawl. The stroke evolved from breaststroke as it also contains a simultaneous leg action and simultaneous arm action. The stroke requires a great deal of upper body strength and can be very physically demanding; therefore, it is a stroke that is swum competitively rather than recreationally.

Buoyancy is significant because the arms recover over the water, and the head raises to breathe; therefore, good floaters will find this far more straightforward than poor floaters.

The undulating action of the body and the legs create great demands on the spine; therefore, swimmers can use many alternative exercises and practices to make learning the stroke easier and less physical.

Breathing is an explosive exhalation and then inhalation in the short second that the head and face are above the water surface.

The timing and coordination of butterfly is a two-beat cycle of leg kicks to one arm cycle. One leg kick should have enough power to assist the upper body out and over the water surface, and the second leg kick should help the arms as they recover just over the water's surface.

Body Position

The body position varies through the stroke cycle due to the continuous undulating action. The body should undulate from head to toe, producing a dolphin-type action. Although undulation is unavoidable, the body position should be kept as horizontal as possible to keep frontal resistance to a minimum. Intermittent or alternative breathing will help to maintain this required body position.

The body should be face down (prone), with the crown of the head leading the action.

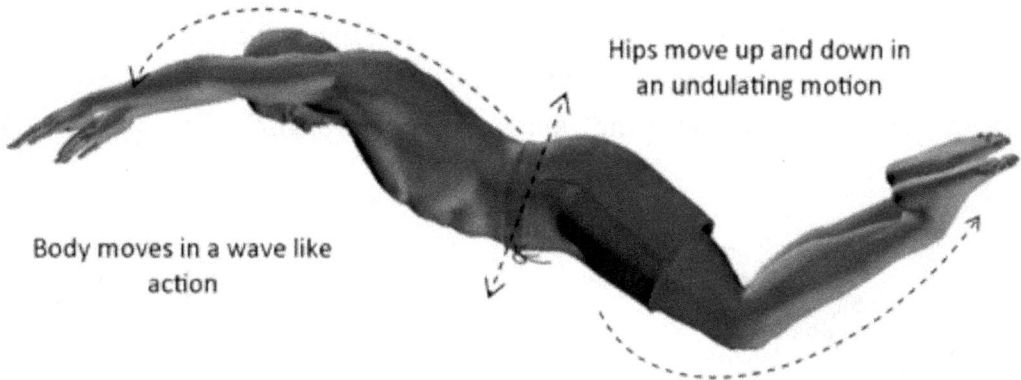

Hips move up and down in an undulating motion

Body moves in a wave like action

The shoulders should remain level throughout, and the head should stay central and still, looking down until breathing is required.

Hips should be in line with the shoulders and should remain parallel to the direction of travel.

Common body position mistakes

The most common mistake made when performing the undulating movement is an excessive movement up and down. As the movement originates from the head, there is a tendency to exaggerate, causing the wave moving through the rest of the body to become excessive and over-pronounced. The swimmer then puts more effort and energy into moving up and down instead of swimming forwards.

A simple push and glide exercise from the poolside followed by a gentle undulating movement across the surface of the water help to eliminate any excessive body movements.

If the swimmer uses the undulation to move forward, this will provide a solid base to build and perfect butterfly stroke.

Leg Kick

The main functions of butterfly stroke leg action are to balance the arm action and help to provide some propulsion. This action then generates the undulating movement of the body position as the swimmer moves through the water.

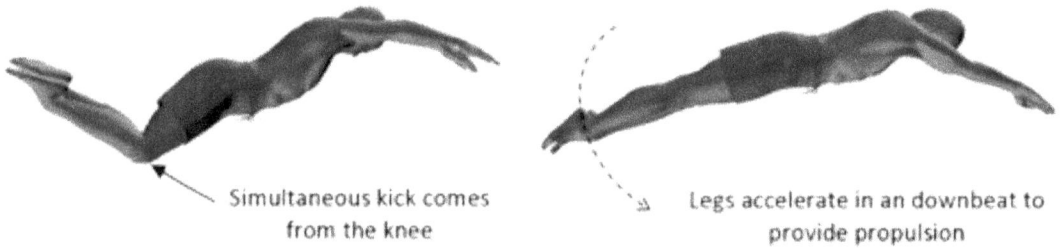

Simultaneous kick comes
from the knee

Legs accelerate in an downbeat to
provide propulsion

The legs kick simultaneously in an action that is similar to that of front crawl but with a greater and more pronounced knee bend.

The upbeat of the kick should come from the hip and the ankles should be relaxed with toes pointed. The legs move upwards without bending at the knees, and the soles of the feet press against the water vertically and backwards.

Knees bend and then straighten on the downbeat to provide propulsion. The legs should accelerate to provide power on the downbeat.

Common leg kick mistakes

A breaststroke type leg kick can sometimes be performed by mistake, due to the simultaneous nature of the kick itself. Most swimmers that are able to perform breaststroke fairly well will naturally kick their legs in a small circle when attempting butterfly leg kick for the first time.

Another common mistake is to place an emphasis on the arm pull for butterfly and therefore lose all power from the leg kick. The legs just go through the motions when in fact they are needed to assist the body to rise out of the water so that the arm pull and recovery can be completed with minimum effort.

A powerful butterfly leg kick is vital and performing the kick whilst holding a float or kickboard out in front with straight arms will help develop the technique and power required for this movement.

Arms

Butterfly arm action is a continuous simultaneous movement that requires significant upper body strength. The action of the arms is similar to front crawl, and the underwater catch, down sweep and upsweep parts, draw the shape of a 'keyhole' through its movement path.

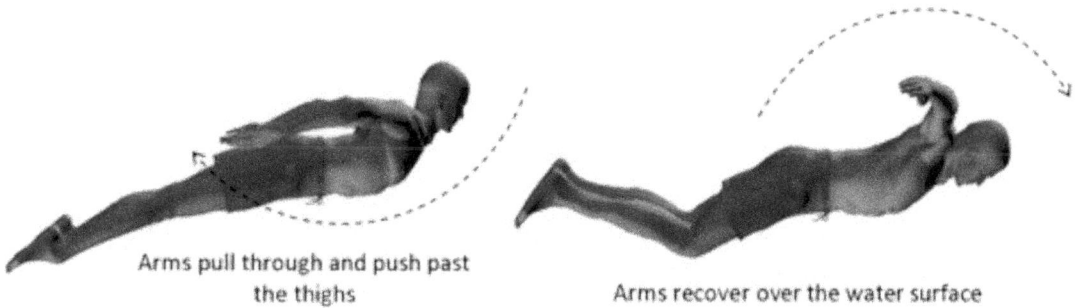

Arms pull through and push past the thighs

Arms recover over the water surface

Entry
The entry of the hands into the water should be fingertips first, leading with the thumb. Fingers should be together with palms flat and facing outwards. The swimmer's arms should be stretched forward with a slightly bent elbow. Entry should be with arms extended in line with the shoulders.

Catch and down sweep

The catch and down sweep should begin just outside the shoulder line. Palms remain facing in the direction of travel, and the elbow should bend to about 90 degrees to provide the extra power required—the hands sweep in a circular motion similar to breaststroke but in a downward path.

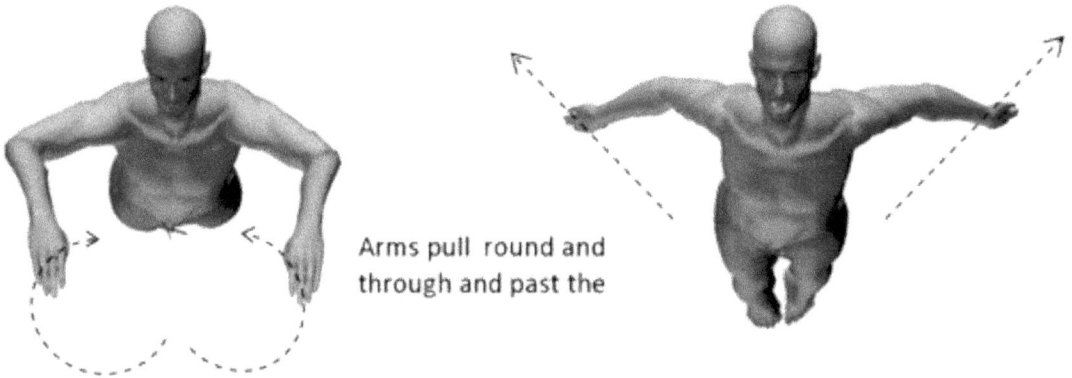

Arms pull round and through and past the

Upsweep

The pitch of the hands changes to face out and upwards towards the water surface. Elbows extend fully to straighten the arms and hands towards the thighs.

Recovery

Hands and arms must clear the water when recovering, and arms and hands should exit the water with little fingers facing upwards. Arms must clear the surface as they are 'thrown' over and forwards. Palms remain facing outwards, naturally giving a thumb-first entry.

Common arm pull mistakes

The two most common mistakes made during butterfly arm technique are an incomplete or short pull and a wide hand entry.

The arm technique is sometimes compared to front crawl when taught to beginners in its most basic form, and this is due to the long sweep and the recovery over the water surface. This is where the similarities end, and this comparison can sometimes be taken literally, resulting in an almost double front crawl arm action with an excessive elbow bend.

A wide hand entry is the most common mistake made amongst slightly more advanced butterfly swimmers. The hands should enter the water in line with the shoulders, and if the entry is wide, this will result in a weak and inefficient arm pull. Simply walking through shallow water of about shoulder depth practising the arm action in slow motion will help establish a full sweep and an inline hand entry.

Breathing

The breathing technique during butterfly is a rapid and explosive action. Inhalation occurs as the arms complete their upsweep and begin to recover as the body starts to rise. The head is lifted enough for the mouth to clear the water, and the chin should be pushed forward but remain at the water surface. Some exhalation underwater takes place during this phase.

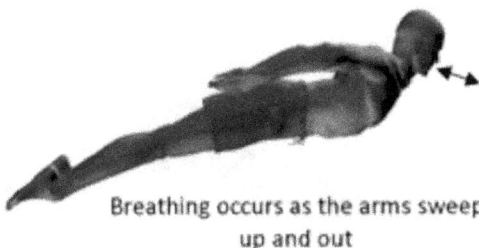

Breathing occurs as the arms sweep up and out

Face submerges at the arms recover

The head is lowered quickly into the water again as the arms recover in line with the shoulders to resume an overall streamlined position and maintain minimal frontal resistance.

Explosive breathing is usually preferred, but swimmers can use a combination of trickle and explosive breathing. Explosive breathing involves a rapid exhalation followed immediately by inhalation, requiring powerful respiratory muscles.

Common breathing mistakes

Failure to breathe is the most common mistake made by beginners learning butterfly breathing techniques.

Because the inhalation and exhalation have to occur very quickly in the short second the face is being raised, it is very common to either inhale only or not breathe at all— the result: a pair of highly inflated lungs a severe lack of oxygen.

Performing the entire stroke and taking a breath every other stroke cycle is a good way of ensuring that exhalation is taking place and that the lungs are sufficiently emptied before inhalation takes place.

Timing

The butterfly stroke cycle should contain two leg kicks to one arm cycle where the first kick occurs when the arms are forward and the second kick when they have pulled back.

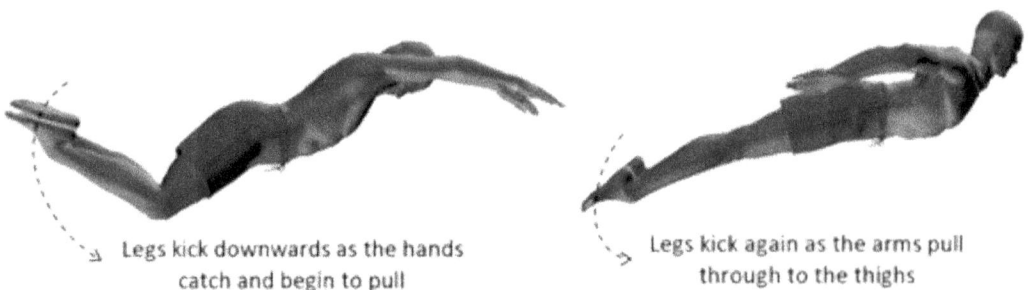

Legs kick downwards as the hands catch and begin to pull

Legs kick again as the arms pull through to the thighs

The downbeat of the first leg kick occurs at the catch and down sweep phase. Both arms will have been in the air during recovery, causing the hips to sink. The subsequent kick should be strong enough to counterbalance this hip movement.

The second downbeat leg kick occurs during the arm cycle's powerful and accelerating upsweep phase. Breathing can occur every stroke cycle or every other stroke cycle.

Common timing mistakes

Timing and coordination issues can occur when the swimmer attempts to kick and pull simultaneously. There should be a delay from the leg kick as the arms pull so that the first powerful leg kick assists the arms recovery. Beginners learning butterfly tend to miss out the second supporting leg kick as the arms recover.

An excellent way to practice and develop the timing for this stroke is to swim using a butterfly leg kick and a breaststroke arm pull. There is less energy used when swimming with breaststroke arms because the arms recover under the water surface. Therefore, it is ideal to ensure that there are two leg kicks for each arm pull, where one leg kick assists the body to rise and breathe, and the other more minor leg kick helps the arms to recover.

Once this exercise is perfected, the swimmer can reintroduce butterfly arms into the stroke and maintain the timing and coordination pattern.

Butterfly Exercises

'I hear and I forget
I see and I remember
I do and I understand'
Confucius

Butterfly Exercises

The lessons plans that follow on from these exercises cover lessons for beginners, intermediate and advanced swimmers. Although these exercises form the foundation from which to teach butterfly, many other exercises are used throughout the lesson plans.

Every swimming teacher has their own 'take' on a particular exercise and many will have more exercises and drills in their repertoire to call upon. Listing all possible butterfly exercises and drills and their variations would be an endless task and therefore beyond the scope of this book.

It is assumed that a swimming teacher will use their professional judgement and experience to make the best use of the exercises and lesson plans outlined here.

Body Position

Holding the poolside

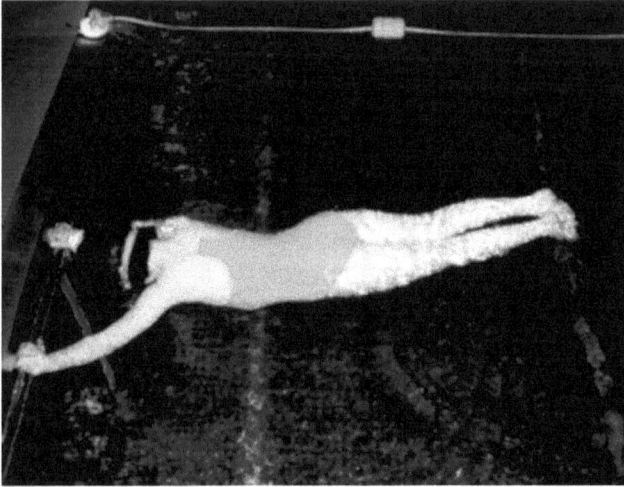

Aim: to practise the body position and movement by holding on to the poolside.

The swimmer performs an undulating action whilst using the poolside or rail for support. **Note:** this exercise should be performed slowly and without force or power as the static nature places pressure on the lower back.

Teaching Points

- Keep your head in the middle
- Make the top of your head lead first
- Keep your shoulders level
- Keep your hips level
- Make your body into a long wave

Teacher's Focus

- Movements should be slow and gradual
- Head remains central
- Shoulders and hips should be level
- Horizontal body with an undulating movement
- Wave like movement from head to toe
- Legs remain together

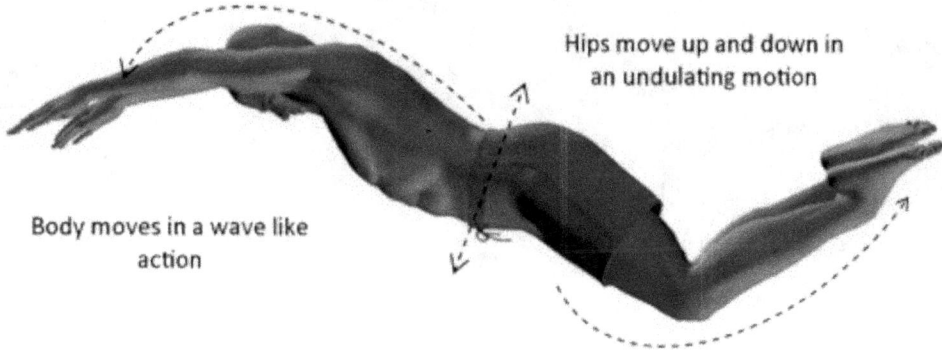

Hips move up and down in an undulating motion

Body moves in a wave like action

Common Faults	Remedy
Body remains too stiff and rigid	Encourage the pupil to relax and repeat
Head moves to the sides	Reiterate the teaching point
Shoulders and hips are not remaining level	Demonstrate and repeat

Body Position

Dolphin dives

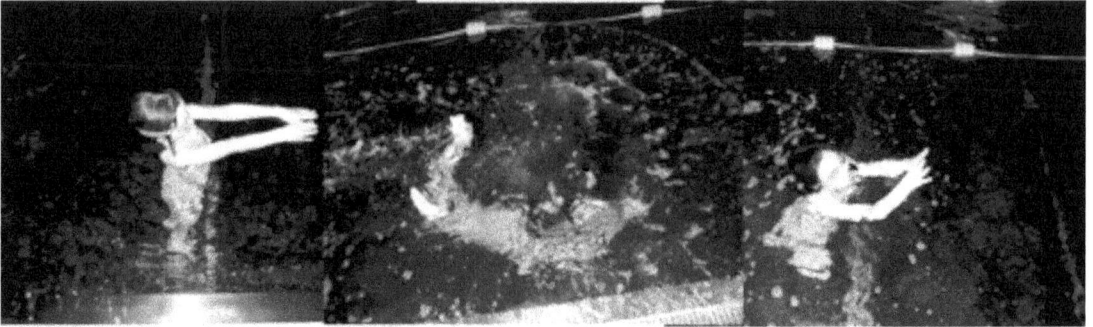

Aim: to develop an undulating body movement whilst travelling through water of standing depth.

The swimmer performs a series of dives from a standing position, diving deep under the surface, arching the back and resurfacing immediately to stand up. The aim is to perform as many dolphin dives across the width as possible. Swimmers can then progress to performing the practice without standing in-between dives.

Teaching Points

- Keep your head in the middle
- Make the top of your head dive down first
- Make your body into a huge wave
- Stretch up to the surface

Teacher's Focus

- Head remains central
- Shoulders and hips should be level
- Body moves with an undulating movement
- Wave-like movement from head to toe
- Legs remain together

Body Position
Dolphin dives

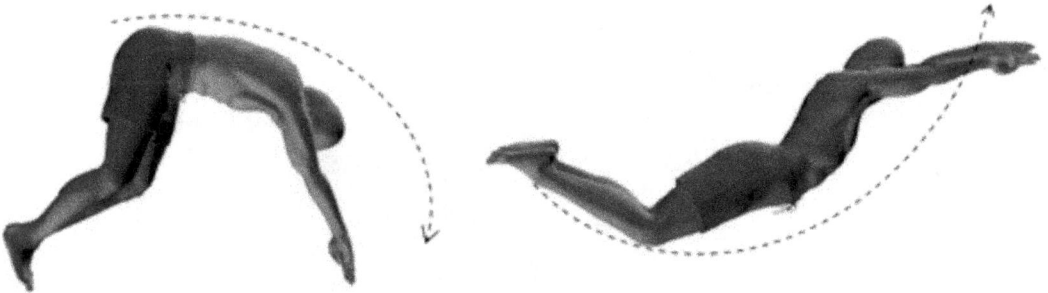

Body dives down and then resurfaces immediately in a wave like movement

Common Faults	Remedy
Body remains too stiff and rigid	Encourage movement to flow
Body dives but fails to undulate upwards	Reiterate the teaching point
Leading with the head looking forwards	Encourage the pupil to focus downwards

Body Position

Push and glide

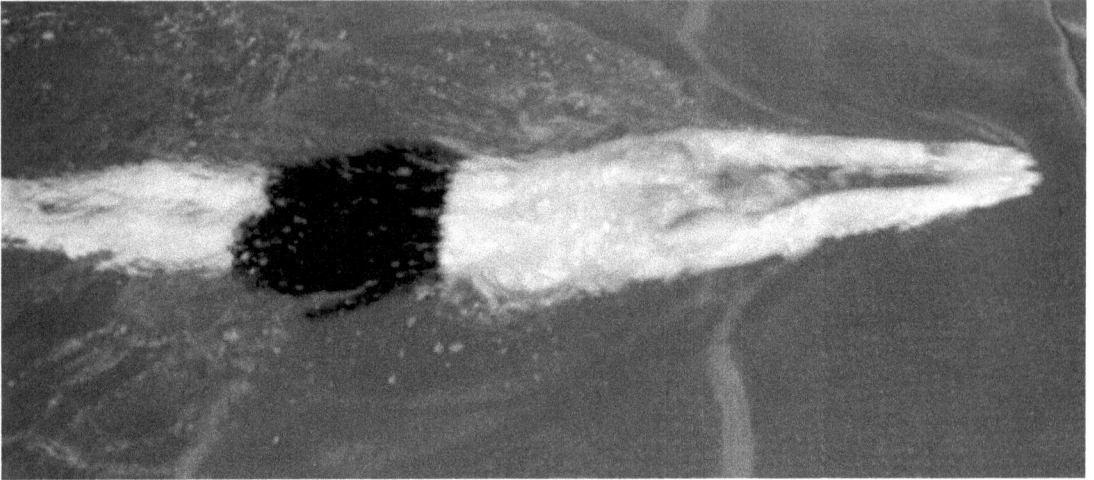

Aim: to practise and develop an undulating action whilst moving.

The swimmer pushes from the poolside into a glide and then begins the undulating action from head to toe. This allows the swimmer to experience the required undulating action whilst moving through the water.

Teaching Points

- Make the top of your head lead first
- Keep your shoulders level
- Keep your hips level
- Make your body into a long wave
- Pretend you are a dolphin swimming

Teacher's Focus

- Head remains central
- Shoulders and hips should be level
- Body is horizontal with an undulating movement
- Wave-like movement from head to toe
- Legs remain together

Legs
Push and glide

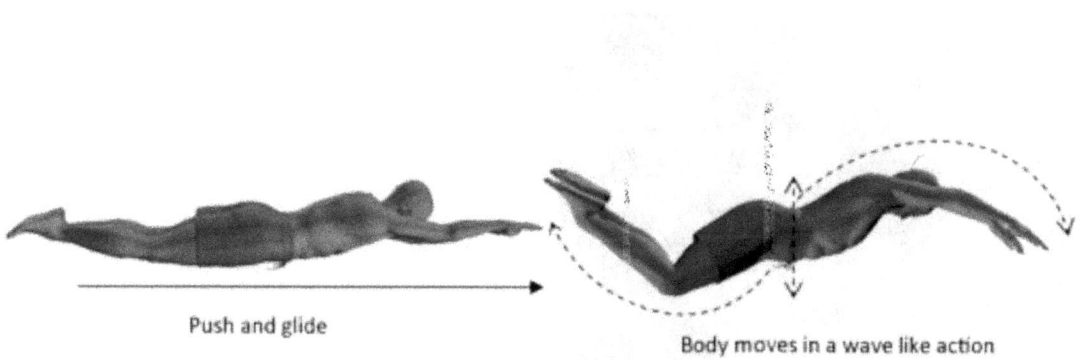

Push and glide

Body moves in a wave like action

Common Faults	Remedy
Body remains too stiff and rigid	Encourage the pupil to relax and repeat
Shoulders and hips are not remaining level	Repeat earlier body position practices
Leading with the head looking forwards	Encourage the pupil to look downwards

Legs

Sitting on the poolside

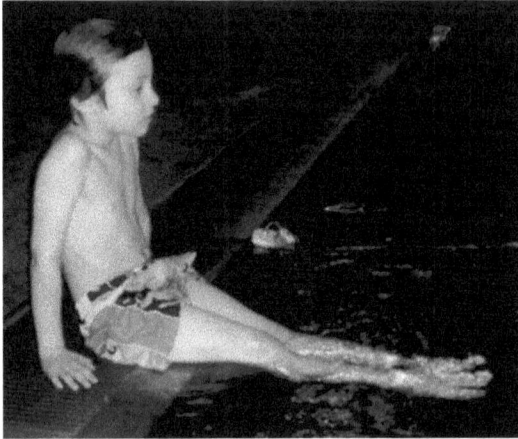

Aim: to develop the kicking action whilst sitting on the poolside.

Bending and kicking from the knees with legs together allows the swimmer to practise the correct movement and feel the water at the same time.

Teaching Points

- Kick both legs at the same time
- Keep your ankles loose
- Keep your legs together
- Point your toes

Teacher's Focus

- Simultaneous legs action
- Knees bend and kick in upbeat to provide propulsion
- Legs accelerate on upbeat
- Toes are pointed

Simultaneous kick comes
from the knee

Toes are pointed

Legs accelerate in an upbeat
though the water

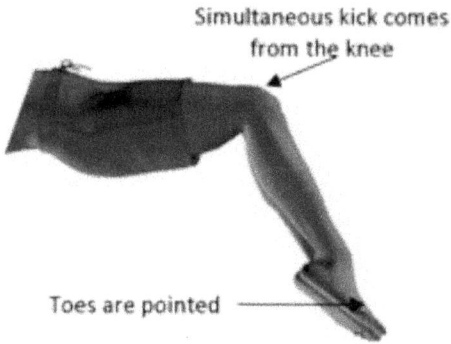

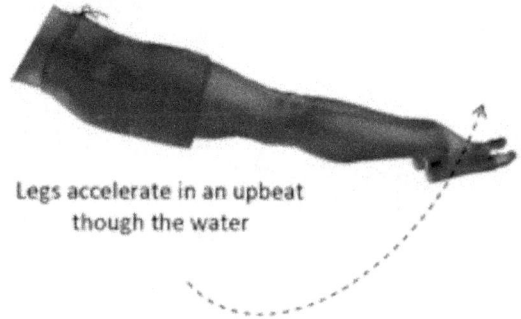

Common Faults	Remedy
Leg kick is not simultaneous	Reiterate the teaching point and repeat
Toes are not pointed	Reiterate the teaching point and repeat
Overall action is too stiff and rigid	Repeat the previous leg practice
Kick is not deep or powerful enough	Reiterate the teaching point and repeat

Legs

Push and glide adding leg kick

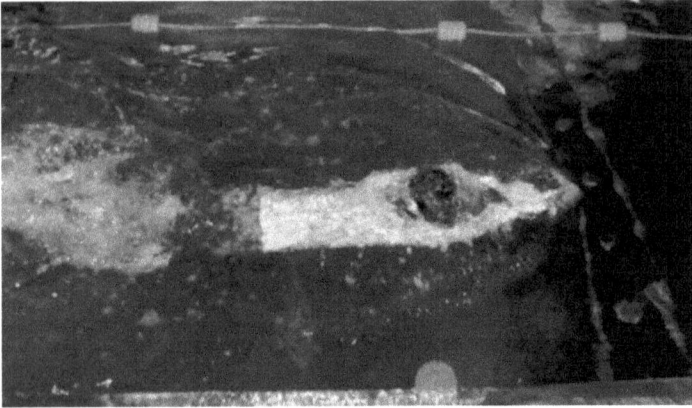

Aim: to practise the dolphin leg kick action and experience movement.

This allows the swimmer the develop propulsion from the accelerating leg kick and undulating body movement.

Teaching Points

- Keep your ankles loose
- Kick downwards powerfully
- Keep your legs together
- Point your toes
- Kick like a mermaid
-

Teacher's Focus

- Simultaneous legs action
- Knees bend and kick in downbeat to provide propulsion
- Legs accelerate on downbeat
- Toes are pointed
- Hips initiate undulating movement

Legs
Push and glide adding leg kick

Simultaneous kick comes
from the knee

Legs accelerate in an downbeat to
provide propulsion

Common Faults	Remedy
Leg kick is not simultaneous	Reiterate the teaching point and repeat
Toes are not pointed	Reiterate the teaching point and repeat
Overall action is too stiff and rigid	Repeat the previous leg practice
Kick is not deep or powerful enough	Reiterate the teaching point and repeat

Legs

Prone holding a float with both hands

Aim: to develop the leg kick using a float for support.

This practice allows the advanced swimmer to develop leg kick strength and stamina as the float isolates the legs.

Teaching Points

- Kick with both legs at the same time
- Kick downwards powerfully
- Keep your legs together
- Create a wave-like action through your body
- Kick like a mermaid

Teacher's Focus

- Simultaneous legs action
- Knees bend and kick in downbeat to provide propulsion
- Legs accelerate on downbeat
- Toes are pointed
- Hips initiate undulating movement

Legs
Prone holding a float with both hands

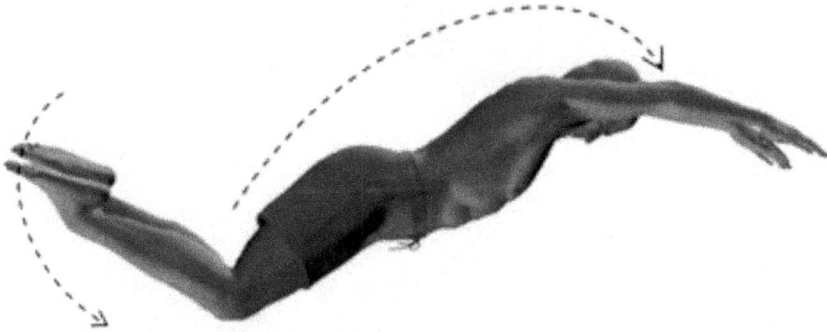

Powerful leg kick provides propulsion and help the body to undulate

Common Faults	Remedy
Leg kick is not simultaneous	Repeat earlier leg practices
Toes are not pointed	Repeat earlier leg practices
Overall action is too stiff and rigid	Encourage the pupil to relax and repeat
Kick is not deep or powerful enough	Reiterate teaching point and repeat

Legs

Supine position with arms by sides

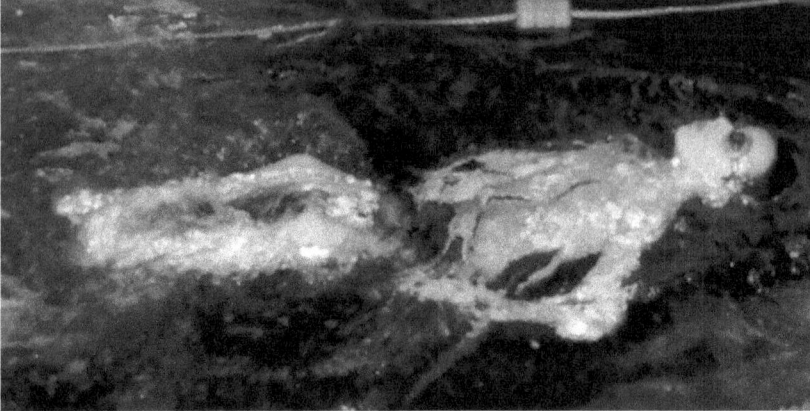

Aim: to practise and develop a dolphin leg kick action in a supine position.

This allows the swimmer to kick continuously whilst facing upwards. This practice requires a great deal of leg strength and stamina and therefore is ideal for developing these aspects of the stroke.

Teaching Points

- Kick both legs at the same time
- Keep your ankles loose
- Kick upwards powerfully
- Keep your legs together
- Point your toes

Teacher's Focus

- Simultaneous leg action
- Knees bend and kick in upbeat to provide propulsion
- Legs accelerate on upbeat
- Toes are pointed
- Hips initiate undulating movement

Legs
Supine position with arms by sides

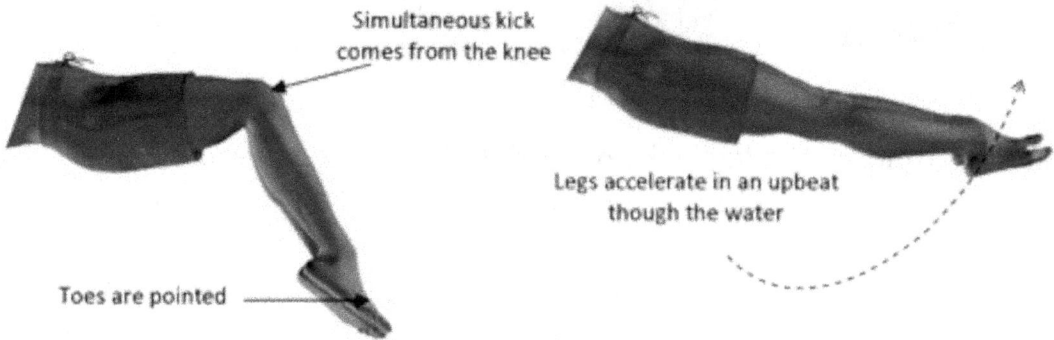

Simultaneous kick comes from the knee

Legs accelerate in an upbeat though the water

Toes are pointed

Common Faults	Remedy
Leg kick is not simultaneous	Repeat earlier leg practices
Overall action is too stiff and rigid	Repeat earlier leg practices
Hips are not undulating to initiate the kick	Repeat previous leg practice
Kick is not deep or powerful enough	Repeat earlier leg practices

Legs

Kick and roll

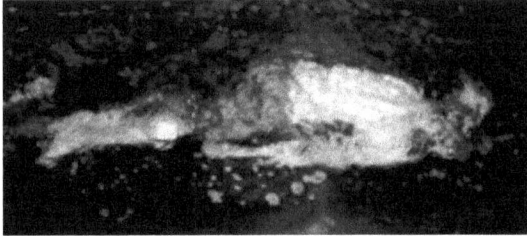

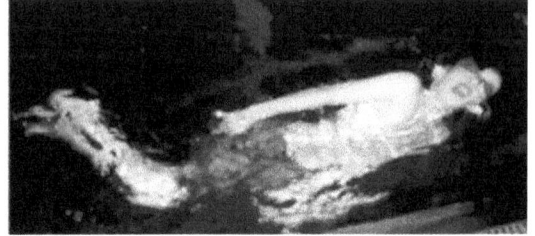

Aim: to combine the leg kick and undulating body movement and perform a rolling motion through the water.

This practice can be performed with arms held by the sides or held out in front. The rolling motion forces the swimmer to use the head, shoulders and hips to produce the movement required for powerful undulating propulsion.

Teaching Points

- Kick both legs at the same time
- Keep your ankles loose
- Roll like a corkscrew
- Keep your legs together
- Make your body snake through the water

Teacher's Focus

- Simultaneous legs action
- Head and shoulders initiate rolling motion
- Knees bend and kick to provide propulsion
- Legs accelerate on downbeat
- Hips initiate undulating movement

Legs kick and body performs a 'cork screw' like roll through the water

Common Faults	Remedy
Leg kick is not simultaneous	Repeat earlier leg practices
Overall action is too stiff and rigid	Reiterate the teaching point and repeat
Kick is not powerful enough	Repeat earlier leg practices

Arms

Standing on the poolside

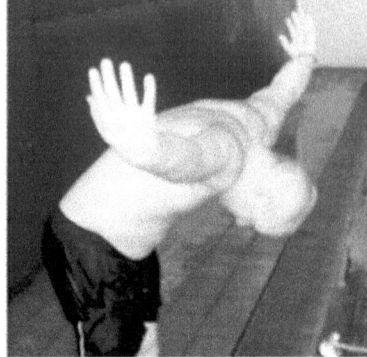

Aim: to practise correct butterfly arm action whilst standing on the poolside.

The pupil is able to work through the arm action slowly and in stages so as to experience the basic movement required.

Teaching Points

- Move both arms at the same time
- Thumbs go in first
- Draw a keyhole under your body
- Push past your thighs

Teacher's Focus

- Arms move simultaneously
- Hands enter the water in line with the shoulders
- Hands pull in the shape of a keyhole
- Hands push past the thigh

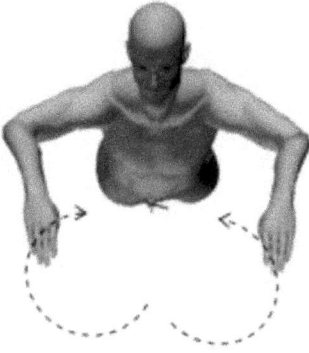

Arms pull through in a keyhole shape

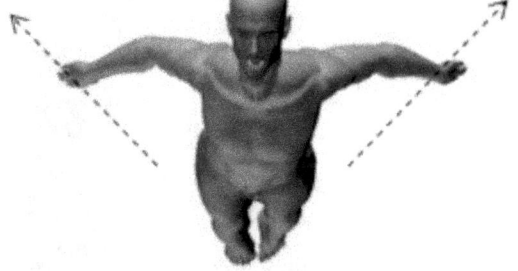

Arms pull through and past the thighs

Common Faults	Remedy
Arm action is not simultaneous	Reiterate the teaching point and repeat
Arms are too straight	Encourage elbow bend and repeat
Arms are not pulling back to the thighs	Reiterate the teaching point and repeat

Arms

Walking on the pool floor

Aim: to progress from the previous practice and develop the arm action.

The swimmer can get a feel for the water whilst walking and performing the simultaneous arm action.

Teaching Points

- Move both arms at the same time
- Thumbs go in first
- Draw a keyhole under your body
- Push past your thighs

Teacher's Focus

- Arms move simultaneously
- Hands enter the water in line with the shoulders
- Hands pull in the shape of a keyhole
- Hands push past the thigh

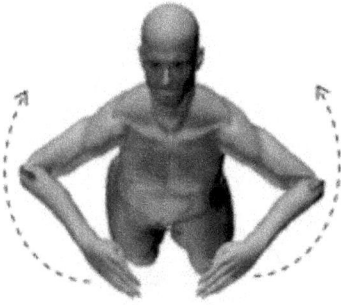

Arms pull through simultaneously

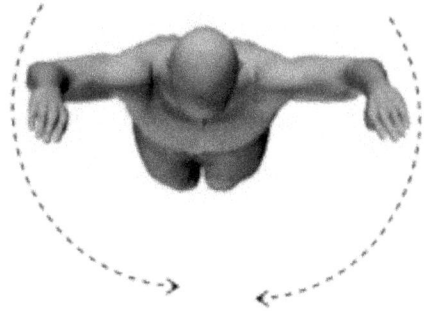

Arms are thrown forwards over the water surface

Common Faults	Remedy
Arm action is not simultaneous	Repeat previous arm practice
Arms are too straight	Demonstrate and repeat
Fingers are apart	Reiterate the teaching point and repeat
Hands fail to clear the water	Reiterate the teaching point and repeat

Arms

Push and glide adding arms

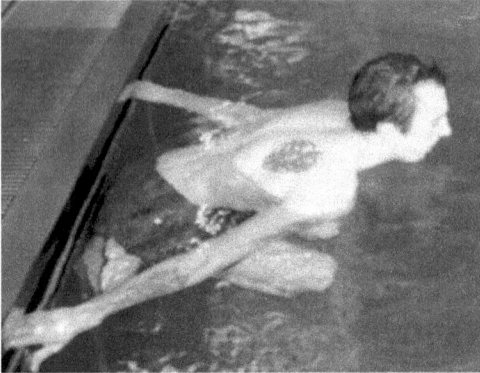

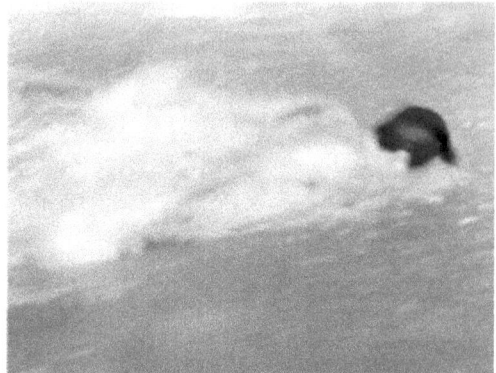

Aim: to practise the arm action whilst moving through the water.

Correct body position is established from the push and glide and the swimmer can then use the arm action to maintain momentum through the water. A limited number of arm pulls can be achieved with this practice.

Teaching Points

- Move both arms at the same time
- Thumbs enter water first
- Pull hard through the water
- Pull past your thighs
- Throw your arms over the water

Teacher's Focus

- Arms move simultaneously
- Fingers closed together
- Thumbs enter the water first
- Hands enter the water in line with the shoulders
- Hands push past the thigh
- Hands clear water surface on recovery

Arms

Push and glide adding arms

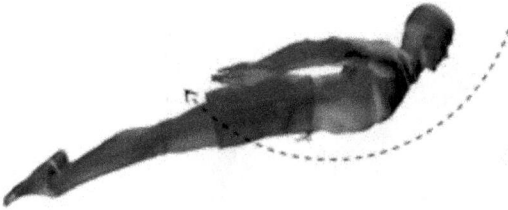

Arms pull through and push past the thighs

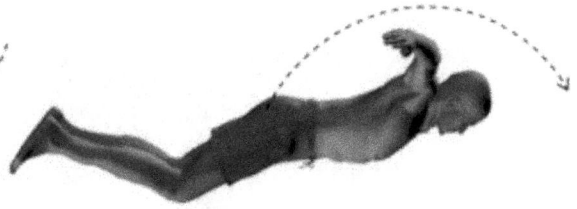

Arms recover over the water surface

Common Faults	Remedy
Arms are too straight	Reiterate the teaching point, demonstrate and practice
Arms are not pulling back to the thighs	Demonstrate and repeat
Hands fail to clear the water	Reiterate the teaching point, demonstrate and practice
Fingers are apart	Reiterate the teaching point, demonstrate and practice

Arms

Arms only using a pull-buoy

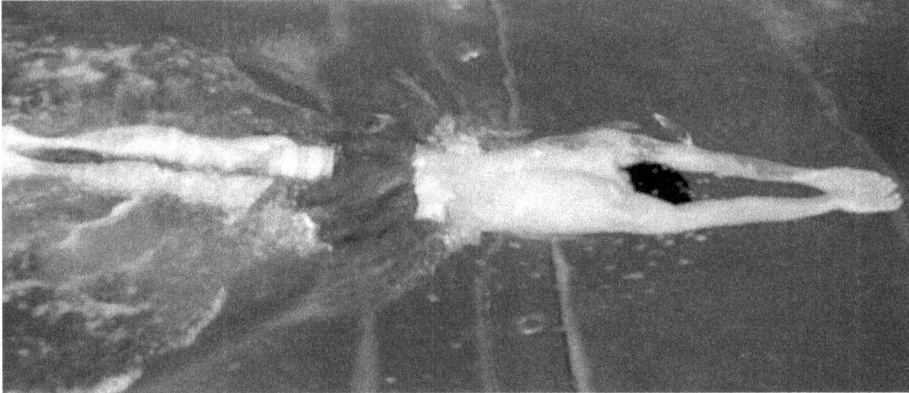

Aim: to help the swimmer develop arm strength and stamina.

This practice is performed over a longer distance, progressing from the previous practice. The pull buoy provides buoyancy and support as well as helps the undulating body movement.

Teaching Points

- Thumbs go in first
- Pull hard through the water
- Pull past your thighs
- Throw your arms over the water

Teacher's Focus

- Arms move simultaneously
- Fingers closed together
- Thumbs enter the water first
- Hands enter the water in line with the shoulders
- Hands push past the thigh
- Hands clear water surface on recovery

Arms

Arms only using a pull-buoy

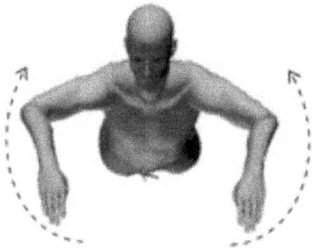

Arms pull through the water with power

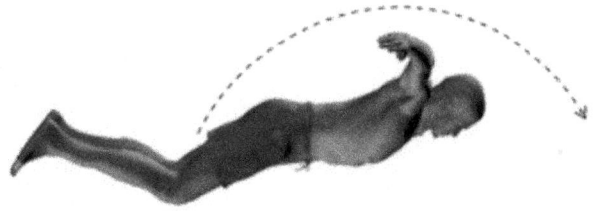

Hands and arms clear the water on recovery

Common Faults	Remedy
Fingers are too wide apart	Reiterate the teaching point, demonstrate and practice
Arms are too straight	Demonstrate and repeat
Arms are not pulling back to the thighs	Repeat earlier arm practices
Hands fail to clear the water	Reiterate teaching point and repeat

Arms

Arm action with breaststroke leg kicks

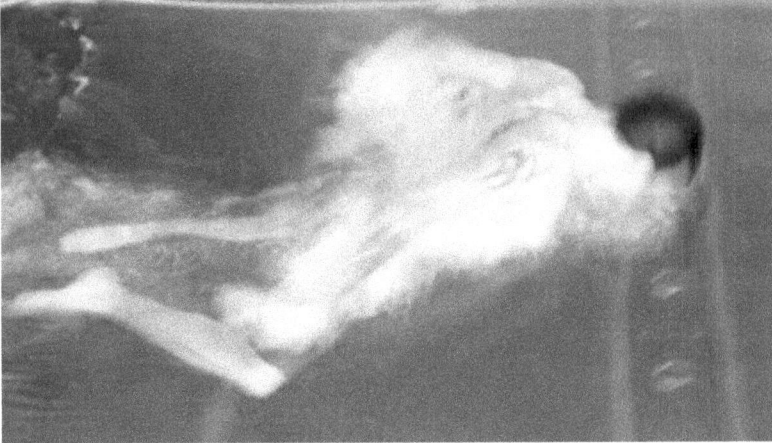

Aim: to enable use of breaststroke leg kicks to support the arm action.

As the legs kick, the propulsion helps the body to rise and the arms to recover over the water surface. This practice is also a good introduction to the timing of butterfly arms and legs.

Teaching Points

- Thumbs go in first
- Draw a keyhole under your body
- Pull past your thighs
- Little finger comes out first
- Throw your arms over the water

Teacher's Focus

- Thumbs enter the water first
- Hands pull in the shape of a keyhole
- Hands push past the thigh
- Little finger exits the water first
- Hands clear water surface on recovery

Arms
Arm action with breaststroke leg kicks

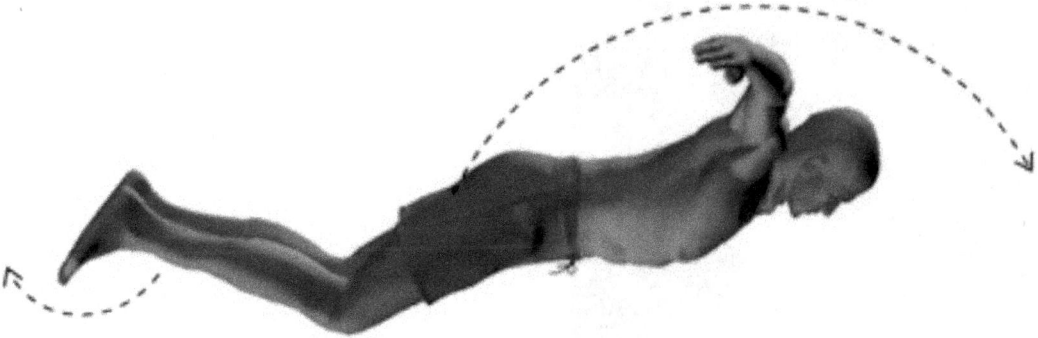

Leg kick help the arms to recover over the water surface

Common Faults	Remedy
Arms are too straight	Demonstrate and repeat
Arms are not pulling back to the thighs	Reiterate the teaching point and repeat
Fingers are apart	Reiterate the teaching point and repeat
Hands fail to clear the water	Reiterate the teaching point and repeat

Breathing

Standing breathing, with arm pulls

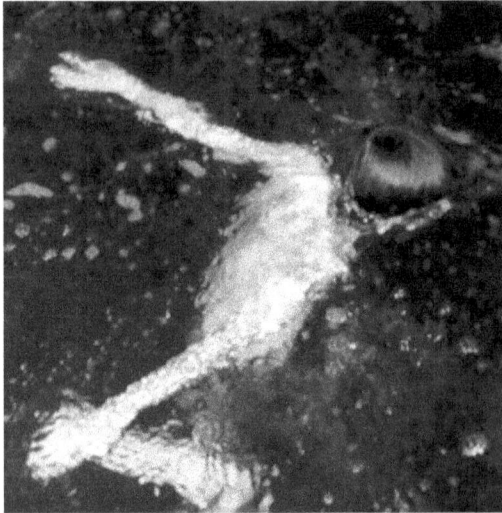

Aim: to incorporate butterfly breathing into the arm action.

This practice is performed standing either on the poolside or stationary in water of standing depth.

Teaching Points

- Blow out hard as your chin rises
- Put your face down as your arms recover
- Push your chin forward and breathe every arm pull or every two arm pulls

Teacher's Focus

- Breathing in should occur as the arms sweep up and out
- Explosive breathing is most beneficial
- Chin should remain in the water
- Face dives into the water as the arms come level with the shoulders
- Breath can be taken every stroke cycle or alternate cycles

Breathing
Standing breathing, with arm pulls

Breathing occurs as the arms sweep up and out

Face submerges at the arms recover

Common Faults	Remedy
Lifting the head too high	Demonstrate and repeat
Arms stop recovery to breathe	Encourage continuous arm action
Holding the breath	Reiterate the teaching point and repeat

Breathing

Full stroke

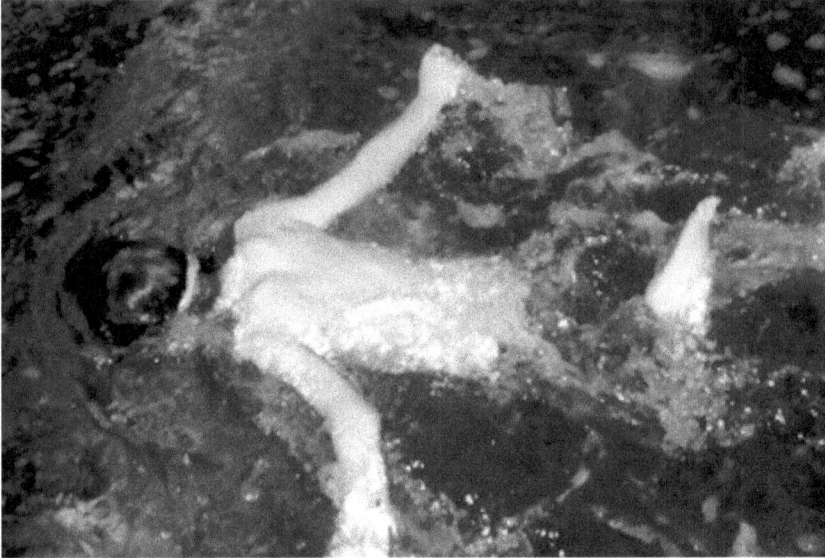

Aim: to use the full stroke to practice breathing, incorporating regular breaths into the arm and leg actions.

Teaching Points

- Blow out hard as your chin rises
- Lift your head to breathe in as your legs kick down
- Put your face down as your arms come over
- Push your chin forward and breathe every arm pull or every two arm pulls

Teacher's Focus

- Breathing in occurs as the arms sweep upwards
- Breathing in occurs as the legs are kicking downwards
- Explosive breathing is most beneficial
- Chin remains in the water
- Face dives into the water as the arms come level with the shoulders
- Breath can be taken every stroke cycle or alternate cycles

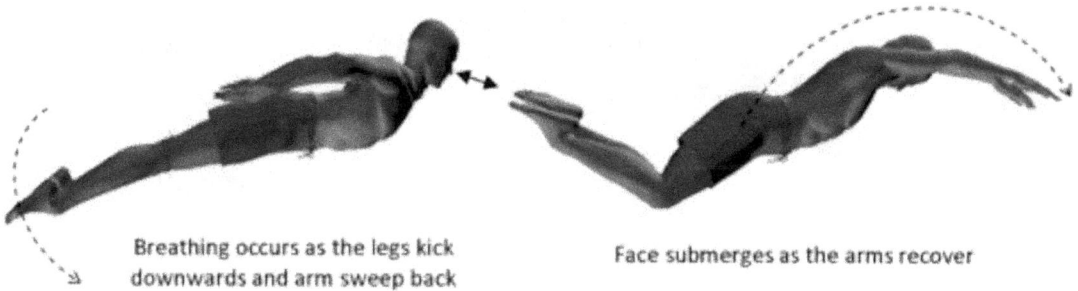

Breathing occurs as the legs kick downwards and arm sweep back

Face submerges as the arms recover

Common Faults	Remedy
Lifting the head too high	Repeat previous breathing practice
Arms stop recovery to breathe	Repeat previous breathing practice
Holding the breath	Reiterate the teaching point and repeat
Breathing too often	Repeat previous breathing practice

Timing

Full stroke

Aim: to perform the full stroke butterfly, incorporating two leg kicks per arm pull.

Teaching Points

- Kick hard as your hands enter the water
- Kick again as your hands pull under your body

Teacher's Focus

- Two legs kicks per arm cycle
- Legs kick once as hands enter and sweep out
- Legs kick once as arms sweep up and out

Legs kick downwards as the hands
catch and begin to pull

Legs kick again as the arms pull
through to the thighs

Common Faults	Remedy
Only kicking once per arm cycle	Reiterate the teaching point, demonstrate and practice
Kicking too many times per arm cycle	Reiterate the teaching point, demonstrate and practice

Lesson Plans

Lesson Plan Layout

> ## Lesson Plan #2
>
> **Lesson type: full stroke front crawl**
> **Level:** adult or child intermediate
> **Previous learning:** basic front crawl technique
> **Lesson aim:** to progress and develop the whole stroke
> **Equipment:** floats, pull buoys, sinkers and hoop

Lesson type: the part of butterfly that this lesson focuses on. For example, **Butterfly Leg Kick**.

Level: who the lesson is aimed at and if they are beginners, intermediate or advanced level. For example, **Child Beginner.**

Previous learning: the aspects of swimming the pupil is expected to have covered before this lesson. For example, **basic front paddle**. The pupil is *not* expected to have completely mastered this aspect of swimming but should have had some experience of learning it.

Lesson aim: the lesson objective or desired outcome of the lesson. For example, 'to learn basic butterfly leg kick and introduce breathing'.

Equipment: the equipment you will need for this lesson. For example, 'floats, buoyancy aids and hoop'.

Lesson Sequences

Lesson plans are laid out in a sequence (beginner, intermediate, advanced) to give the teacher easy reference to other lessons, exercises and activities in the sequence. This should allow for easier differentiation across varying abilities.

Lesson plans do not have to be followed in sequence, although they can be if you wish. Each plan has its own aim and therefore can be used in sequence with other lessons aimed at that level, to suit the individual pupil or pupils.

These lesson plans and the exercises and activities in them are set out as a guide. Every pupil is different and will interpret and respond to exercises and teaching points in their own way, therefore as a swimming teacher it is important to be flexible in your approach. In other words, where a pupil is finding a particular exercise difficult, chose an easier exercise from a previous plan. Where a pupil is not quite grasping the concept of what you are teaching, try using a different phrase or teaching point.

Teaching Points

Teaching points are our 'magic words'. Having a variety of them in our virtual tool kit can be extremely useful. For example, when you say to a pupil 'point your toes and they just don't get it, you change the teaching point to 'kick with floppy feet'. All of sudden they are kicking with relaxed ankles and pointed toes.

Learning to be creative with our teaching points can be a very powerful skill and can be the difference between a pupil struggling and that light bulb moment when they suddenly understand and can do it.

Organising Your Swimmers

The way you chose to organise your swimmers as they swim off to perform a given exercise is vital to maintaining a safe learning environment and to monitor their progress.

The organisation column of the lesson plans make a suggestion but you will have to use your professional judgement, based on the size of your class and swimming lesson area available in your pool.

The suggestions are:

All together - you instruct all swimmers to go at the same time. Ideal if you have sufficient space and can be unsafe if you do not.

Waves - number your swimmers 1 and 2 alternately (or more if you have a large class). Then instruct all numbers 1's to go first, followed by the number 2's and so on if you have more. This is a good way of monitoring swimmers and also a great way to organise large classes of advanced swimmers.

One-by-one - sending each swimmer off one at a time. This is an ideal way to closely monitor each pupil.

Getting The Timing Right

All swimming pools vary in their dimensions and often larger pools have an area roped off for swimming lessons, so the whole pool is rarely used. These plans assume that beginner and intermediate swimmers will swim widths and advanced swimmers will swim lengths. The size of the width and length in *your* pool might not fit with how these plans are formatted and you may wish to use your professional judgment to change them to fit with your circumstances.

The duration of most swimming lessons is about 30 minutes. The timings of each exercise in these lesson plans are a guide and again, your professional judgement can be used to adjust them to suit your pupils and your pool size.

If you begin to discover that you are racing through the lesson and will have time left over, remember any exercise can be repeated. Repeating an exercise will enhance a pupil's strength, stamina and overall ability. A different teaching point can also be used to help those that perhaps did not quite get it the first time around.

Important Terminology:

Prone - 'facing downwards'. For example, a prone push and glide is performed in the face-down position.

Supine - 'facing downwards' For example, a supine star float is performed on the back, facing upwards.

'By failing to prepare
you are preparing to fail.'
Benjamin Franklin

Lesson Plan #1

Lesson type: full stroke butterfly
Level: adult or child beginner
Previous learning: basic front paddle
Lesson aim: to learn the basics of butterfly and experience the whole stroke
Equipment: woggle, buoyancy aids if needed and hoop

Exercise/Activity	Teaching Points	Organisation	Duration
Entry: swivel or steps entry	enter slowly	all together	1 min
Warm up: 2 widths any stroke with buoyancy aids if needed	take your time	all together	3 mins
Main Theme: standing on the poolside showing hip movement	pretend you are a belly dancer	all together	2 mins
push and glide adding leg kicks, use a woggle if needed	legs together	waves	3 mins
push and glide adding arm pulls	arms enter together	waves	3 mins
push and glide with woggle if needed - add arms, legs and breathing	blow out into the water	waves	3 mins
push and glide adding arm pulls and leg kicks	2 kicks to one arm pull	waves	3 mins
2 widths full stroke butterfly	kick and pull continuously	waves	3 mins
Contrasting Activity: prone star float	deep breath and relax	2 or 3 at a time	3 mins
sitting dive through a hoop at the surface	head tucked down	2 or 3 at a time	3 mins
Exit: using the pool steps or over the poolside	take your time	one by one	1 min

Total time: 28 minutes

Lesson #1 Assessment

Lesson Objective: to learn each part of basic butterfly and experience the whole stroke.

Below average	Average	Above average
😐	🙂	😎
Attempts to demonstrate but does not show the correct technique	Able to perform most of the technique correctly some of the time	Performs the technique correctly most of the time

Assessment	😐	🙂	😎
Face is submerged			
Hips attempt to undulate			
Legs kick together			
Arms enter together			
Attempts 2 kicks to 1 arm pull			

Lesson Plan #2

Lesson type: full stroke butterfly

Level: adult or child intermediate
Previous learning: basic butterfly technique
Lesson aim: to progress and develop the whole stroke to an intermediate level
Equipment: woggle, pull buoy, sinkers and hoop

Exercise/Activity	Teaching Points	Organisation	Duration
Entry: swivel or sitting dive entry	enter slowly	waves	1 min
Warm up: 2 widths any stroke	take your time	all together	2 mins
Main Theme: 2 widths full stroke butterfly with buoyancy aids if needed	pull and kick continuously	waves	3 mins
push and glide adding hip movements	move like a mermaid	one by one	3 mins
leg kicks, using a woggle under the body if needed	slight knee bend	waves	3 mins
arm pulls without kicking, using a woggle if needed	thumb and finger enter first	waves	3 mins
push and glide adding arm pulls and leg kicks	kick your arms in, then kick your arms out	waves	3 mins
full stroke butterfly without buoyancy aids	your head leads the movement	waves	3 mins
Contrasting Activity: head first surface dives, collecting sinkers placed apart	deep breath and dig down	one by one	3 mins
dolphin kick through a hoop at the surface	swim like a mermaid	one by one	3 mins
Exit: using the pool steps or over the poolside	take your time	one by one	1 min

Total time: 28 minutes

Lesson #2 Assessment

Lesson Objective: to progress and develop the whole stroke to an intermediate level.		
Below average	**Average**	**Above average**
😐	🙂	😎
Attempts to demonstrate but does not show the correct technique	Able to perform most of the technique correctly some of the time	Performs the technique correctly most of the time

Assessment	😐	🙂	😎
Undulating movement comes from the head			
Hips undulate continuously			
Legs kick with a slight knee bend			
Hands enter finger and thumb first			
Attempts to 'kick, pull, kick, recover'			

Lesson Plan #3

Lesson type: full stroke butterfly
Level: adult or child advanced
Previous learning: full stroke butterfly
Lesson aim: to develop and fine-tune technique for the whole stroke
Equipment: floats

Exercise/Activity	Teaching Points	Organisation	Duration
Entry: sitting or shallow dive entry	take your time	waves	1 min
Warm up: 2 lengths any stroke	take your time	all together	3 mins
Main Theme: 2 lengths full stroke butterfly	smooth strokes	waves	2 mins
push and glide underwater, adding undulating movement	head leads the movement	waves	3 mins
kicking with arms extended, using fins	move like a dolphin tail	waves	3 mins
arm action using fins on the feet	pull with power	waves	3 mins
full stroke, breathing every stroke	pull your head up	waves	3 mins
2 lengths full stroke butterfly	kick, pull, kick, recover	waves	3 mins
Contrasting Activity: feet-first surface dives to collect an object	stretch up and then sink	waves	3 mins
treading water	head above the water	waves	3 mins
Exit: using the pool steps or over the poolside	take your time	one by one	1 min

Total time: 28 minutes

Lesson #3 Assessment

Lesson Objective: to develop and fine-tune technique for the whole stroke.		
Below average	**Average**	**Above average**
😐	🙂	😎
Attempts to demonstrate but does not show the correct technique	Able to perform most of the technique correctly some of the time	Performs the technique correctly most of the time

Assessment	😐	🙂	😎
Undulating movement comes from the head			
Legs kick continuously and with power			
Hands enter finger and thumb first			
Arms recover low over the water surface			
inhalation takes place as the arms outsweep			
Timing pattern follows 'kick, pull, kick, recover'			

Lesson Plan #4

Lesson type: butterfly body position
Level: adult or child beginner
Previous learning: basic front paddle and push and glide
Lesson aim: to learn basic body position and movement
Equipment: buoyancy aids if needed

Exercise/Activity	Teaching Points	Organisation	Duration
Entry: swivel entry	enter slowly	all together	1 min
Warm up: 2 widths any stroke using buoyancy aids	slow and gentle swim	all together	3 mins
Main Theme: standing on the poolside showing hip movement	pretend you are a belly dancer	all together	2 mins
holding the poolside, slow dolphin kick action	make your body into a long wave	all together	2 mins
dolphin dives whilst walking though the water	stretch up to the surface	waves	4 mins
push and glide with arms by the sides, adding undulating movement	lead with your head	waves	3 mins
push and glide adding dolphin kicks	pretend you are a dolphin	waves	3 mins
2 widths dolphin kick, arms by the sides	face down	waves	3 mins
Contrasting Activity: supine push and glide	feet together and toes pointed	waves	2 mins
sitting dive	head tucked down	one by one	3 mins
Exit: using the pool steps or over the poolside	take your time	one by one	1 min

Total time: 27minutes

80

Lesson #4 Assessment

Lesson Objective: to learn basic butterfly body position and movement.		
Below average	**Average**	**Above average**
😐	🙂	😎
Attempts to demonstrate but does not show the correct technique	Able to perform most of the technique correctly some of the time	Performs the technique correctly most of the time

Assessment	😐	🙂	😎
Body moves in a wave-like action			
Head leads the movement			
Legs and feet are together			
Hips are level			
Shoulders are level			

Lesson Plan #5

Lesson type: butterfly body position
Level: adult or child intermediate
Previous learning: basic butterfly butterfly technique
Lesson aim: to improve basic butterfly body position and movement
Equipment: buoyancy aids if needed and hoop

Exercise/Activity	Teaching Points	Organisation	Duration
Entry: swivel entry	enter slowly	all together	1 min
Warm up: 2 widths any stroke without using buoyancy aids	take your time	all together	3 mins
Main Theme: 2 widths full stroke butterfly	continuous arms and legs	waves	3 mins
dolphin dives whilst walking though the water	stretch up to the surface	waves	3 mins
push and glide with arms by the sides, adding undulating movement	lead with your head	waves	3 mins
supine push and glide with arms by the sides, adding undulating movement	make your hips undulate	waves	3 mins
push and glide with arms extended, adding dolphin kicks	pretend you are a dolphin	waves	3 mins
2 widths full stroke butterfly	continuous arms and legs	waves	3 mins
Contrasting Activity: forward somersault from a push and glide	tuck chin on chest	2 or 3 at a time	3 mins
sitting dive through a submerged hoop	hands together	2 or 3 at a time	3 mins
Exit: using the pool steps or over the poolside	take your time	one by one	1 min

Total time: 29 minutes

Lesson #5 Assessment

Lesson Objective: to improve basic butterfly body position and movement.		
Below average	**Average**	**Above average**
😐	🙂	😎
Attempts to demonstrate but does not show the correct technique	Able to perform most of the technique correctly some of the time	Performs the technique correctly most of the time

Assessment	😐	🙂	😎
Head leads the movement			
Body movement is undulating			
Legs and feet are together			
Hands are together when extended			
Hips and shoulders are level			

Lesson Plan #6

Lesson type: butterfly body position
Level: adult or child advanced
Previous learning: full stroke butterfly
Lesson aim: to develop and fine-tune butterfly body position and movement
Equipment: buoyancy aids if needed

Exercise/Activity	Teaching Points	Organisation	Duration
Entry: sitting or shallow dive entry	take your time	all together	1 min
Warm up: 2 lengths any stroke	steady pace	all together	3 mins
Main Theme: 2 lengths full stroke butterfly	let the stroke flow	all together	3 mins
push and glide with arms extended, adding undulating movement	make your hips undulate	waves	3 mins
supine push and glide with arms extended, adding undulating movement	wave-like body movement	waves	3 mins
push and glide underwater with arms extended, adding dolphin kicks	pretend you are a dolphin	waves	3 mins
push and glide adding leg kicks, measure distance covered	maintain a streamlined shape	waves	3 mins
2 lengths full stroke butterfly from racing start	let your head drive the body action	waves	3 mins
Contrasting Activity: prone push and glide and rotate to supine position	keep head level	2 or 3 at a time	3 mins
any stroke with somersault mid swim	head down, chin to chest	2 or 3 at a time	3 mins
Exit: using the pool steps or over the poolside	take your time	all together	1 min

Total time: 29 minutes

Lesson #6 Assessment

Lesson Objective: to develop and fine-tune butterfly body position and movement.		
Below average	**Average**	**Above average**
😐	🙂	😎
Attempts to demonstrate but does not show the correct technique	**Able to perform most of the technique correctly some of the time**	**Performs the technique correctly most of the time**

Assessment	😐	🙂	😎
Head leads the movement			
Body movement is continuous and undulating			
Legs and feet are together			
Hands are together when extended			
Hips and shoulders are level			
Body movement is smooth and flowing			

Lesson Plan #7

Lesson type: butterfly leg kick
Level: adult or child beginner
Previous learning: basic front paddle and submerging
Lesson aim: to learn basic dolphin kick action
Equipment: floats and buoyancy aids if needed

Exercise/Activity	Teaching Points	Organisation	Duration
Entry: swivel entry	enter slowly	all together	1 min
Warm up: 2 widths any stroke using buoyancy aids	slow and gentle swim	all together	3 mins
Main Theme: sitting on the poolside, legs in the water	kick out like you are on a swing	all together	2 mins
holding the poolside, slow dolphin kick action	kick like a mermaid	all together	2 mins
dolphin leg kicks - holding a float if needed	show your dolphin tail	waves	3 mins
push and glide adding dolphin kicks	kick with both legs together	waves	3 mins
dolphin kick in a supine position	flick your feet upwards	waves	3 mins
2 widths dolphin kick, arms by the sides	face down	waves	3 mins
Contrasting Activity: supine star float	relax and stretch	all together	2 mins
pencil jump	jump outwards	one by one	2 mins
Exit: using the pool steps or over the poolside	take your time	one by one	1 min

Total time: 25 minutes

Lesson #7 Assessment

Lesson Objective: to learn basic dolphin kick action.		
Below average	**Average**	**Above average**
😐	🙂	😎
Attempts to demonstrate but does not show the correct technique	Able to perform most of the technique correctly some of the time	Performs the technique correctly most of the time

Assessment	😐	🙂	😎
Legs kicks are simultaneous			
Toes are pointed			
Legs remain together			
Kick comes from body movement			

Lesson Plan #8

Lesson type: butterfly leg kick
Level: adult or child intermediate
Previous learning: basic butterfly technique
Lesson aim: to strengthen and develop basic butterfly leg kick
Equipment: buoyancy aids if needed and hoop

Exercise/Activity	Teaching Points	Organisation	Duration
Entry: swivel or sitting dive entry	enter slowly	all together	1 min
Warm up: 2 widths any stroke	take your time	all together	3 mins
Main Theme: 2 widths full stroke butterfly	let the stroke flow	waves	2 mins
push and glide adding dolphin kicks	kick with both legs together	waves	3 mins
dolphin kick in a supine position	flick your feet upwards	waves	3 mins
kick and roll, arms by the sides	head leads the movement	waves	3 mins
2 widths dolphin kick, arms extended	kick with power	waves	3 mins
2 widths full stroke butterfly	relaxed, flowing kicks	waves	3 mins
Contrasting Activity: sitting dives	chin to chest	one by one	3 mins
push and glide through a submerged hoop	hands and feet together	one by one	3 mins
Exit: using the pool steps	take your time	one by one	1 min

Total time: 28 minutes

Lesson #8 Assessment

Lesson Objective: to strengthen and develop basic butterfly leg kick.		
Below average	**Average**	**Above average**
😐	🙂	😎
Attempts to demonstrate but does not show the correct technique	**Able to perform most of the technique correctly some of the time**	**Performs the technique correctly most of the time**

Assessment	😐	🙂	😎
Legs kicks are simultaneous with legs together			
Toes are pointed with ankles relaxed			
Legs kick with power			
Kick comes from body movement			

Lesson Plan #9

Lesson type: butterfly leg kick
Level: adult or child advanced
Previous learning: full stroke butterfly
Lesson aim: to develop and perfect butterfly leg kick
Equipment: kickboards if needed and fins

Exercise/Activity	Teaching Points	Organisation	Duration
Entry: sitting or shallow dive entry	take your time	waves	1 min
Warm up: 2 lengths any stroke	take your time	all together	3 mins
Main Theme: 2 lengths full stroke butterfly	smooth flowing movements	waves	3 mins
push and glide adding dolphin kicks with arms extended	kick like a dolphin tail	waves	3 mins
dolphin kick with fins	kick with power	waves	3 mins
dolphin kick on the side with arms extended - add optional fins	flick your feet	waves	3 mins
supine dolphin kick with arms extended - add optional fins	slight bend of the knees	waves	3 mins
2 widths full stroke butterfly	relaxed, flowing kicks	waves	3 mins
Contrasting Activity: push and glide into forward somersault	arms pull down to rotate	2 or 3 at a time	2 mins
supine push and glide into somersault	tuck chin to chest	2 or 3 at a time	2 mins
Exit: using the pool steps	take your time	waves	1 min

Total time: 27 minutes

Lesson #9 Assessment

Lesson Objective: to develop and perfect butterfly leg kick.		
Below average	**Average**	**Above average**
😐	🙂	😎
Attempts to demonstrate but does not show the correct technique	Able to perform most of the technique correctly some of the time	Performs the technique correctly most of the time

Assessment	😐	🙂	😎
Toes are pointed with ankles relaxed			
Knee bend is minimal			
Legs kick with power			
Kick comes from body movement			
Kicks are smooth and flowing			

Lesson Plan #10

Lesson type: butterfly arms
Level: adult or child beginner
Previous learning: basic front paddle
Lesson aim: to learn basic butterfly arm action
Equipment: floats, buoyancy aids and hoop

Exercise/Activity	Teaching Points	Organisation	Duration
Entry: swivel entry	enter slowly	all together	1 min
Warm up: 2 widths any stroke using buoyancy aids	slow and gentle swim	all together	3 mins
Main Theme: standing on the poolside, basic arm movement	both arms at the same time	all together	2 mins
walking through water, basic arm movement	pull back together	all together	3 mins
push and glide adding arm movements	make a keyhole shape	waves	3 mins
push and glide adding arm and leg movements	thumb enters first	waves	3 mins
supine dolphin kick adding double arms	kick and pull	waves	3 mins
2 widths full stroke	pull and kick with power	waves	3 mins
Contrasting Activity: sitting dive though a surface hoop	chin tucked down	one by one	3 mins
sitting dive though a submerged hoop	push off and stretch	one by one	3 mins
Exit: using the pool steps or over the poolside	take your time	one by one	1 min

Total time: 28 minutes

Lesson #10 Assessment

Lesson Objective: to learn and practice basic butterfly arm pull.		
Below average	**Average**	**Above average**
🙂	🙂	😎
Attempts to demonstrate but does not show the correct technique	**Able to perform most of the technique correctly some of the time**	**Performs the technique correctly most of the time**

Assessment	🙂	🙂	😎
Arm pulls are simultaneous			
Hand enters the water thumb and finger first			
Fingers are together			
Arms recover simultaneously			

Lesson Plan #11

Lesson type: butterfly arms
Level: adult or child intermediate
Previous learning: basic butterfly technique
Lesson aim: to develop and progress butterfly arm technique
Equipment: buoyancy aids if need, fins and sinkers

Exercise/Activity	Teaching Points	Organisation	Duration
Entry: swivel entry or sitting dive entry	take your time	all together	1 min
Warm up: 2 widths any stroke	continuous swimming	all together	2 mins
Main Theme: 2 widths full stroke butterfly	relaxed, smooth movements	waves	3 mins
push and glide adding arm movements	thumb enters first	waves	3 mins
push and glide adding arm pulls with an underwater recovery	make a keyhole shape	waves	3 mins
push and glide adding arm pulls, kicking with fins to add support	hands accelerate through the water	waves	3 mins
2 widths kicking adding arm pulls (with optional fins)	arms recover low over the water	waves	3 mins
2 widths full stroke butterfly	arms and legs move together	waves	3 mins
Contrasting Activity: treading water	mouth and nose out of the water	one by one	2 mins
retrieve an object from the pool floor and return it to the poolside	eyes open	one by one	4 mins
Exit: using the pool steps or over the poolside	take your time	one by one	1 min

Total time: 28 minutes

Lesson #11 Assessment

Lesson Objective: to develop and progress basic butterfly arm action.		
Below average	**Average**	**Above average**
😐	🙂	😎
Attempts to demonstrate but does not show the correct technique	Able to perform most of the technique correctly some of the time	Performs the technique correctly most of the time

Assessment	😐	🙂	😎
Arm pulls are simultaneous			
Hand enter in line with the shoulders			
Hands pull in a keyhole shape			
Arms recover low over the water surface			
Fingers remain together throughout			

Lesson Plan #12

Lesson type: butterfly arms
Level: adult or child advanced
Previous learning: full stroke butterfly
Lesson aim: to develop and fine-tune butterfly arm action
Equipment: hand paddles and fins if needed

Exercise/Activity	Teaching Points	Organisation	Duration
Entry: sitting or shallow dive entry	take your time	waves	1 min
Warm up: 2 lengths any stroke	take your time	all together	3 mins
Main Theme: 2 lengths full stroke butterfly	let your movements flow	waves	3 mins
push and glide adding arm movements, counting arm pull over a short distance	hands enter inline with shoulders	waves	3 mins
push and glide adding arm pulls, using hand paddles	hands accelerate through the water	waves	3 mins
2 widths kicking adding arm pulls, counting arm pulls (with optional fins)	arms recover low over the water	waves	3 mins
Repeat previous drill maintaining or reducing number of arm pulls	fast and relaxed arm action	waves	3 mins
2 widths full stroke butterfly	smooth flowing movements	waves	3 mins
Contrasting Activity: feet first sculling	feet remain at the surface	waves	3 mins
basic racing start	head tucked down on entry	one at a time	3 mins
Exit: using the pool steps or over the poolside	take your time	waves	1 min

Total time: 29 minutes

Lesson #12 Assessment

Lesson Objective: to develop and fine-tune butterfly arm action.		
Below average	**Average**	**Above average**
😐	🙂	😎
Attempts to demonstrate but does not show the correct technique	**Able to perform most of the technique correctly some of the time**	**Performs the technique correctly most of the time**

Assessment	😐	🙂	😎
Arm pulls are relaxed and continuous			
Hands accelerate though the water			
Hands pull in a keyhole shape			
Arms recover low over the water surface			
Hands enter in line with the shoulders			

Lesson Plan #13

Lesson type: butterfly breathing
Level: adult or child beginner
Previous learning: front paddle, including breathing and submerging
Lesson aim: to learn basic butterfly breathing technique
Equipment: buoyancy aids if needed

Exercise/Activity	Teaching Points	Organisation	Duration
Entry: swivel entry	enter slowly	all together	1 min
Warm up: 2 widths any stroke using buoyancy aids	slow and gentle swim	all together	3 mins
Main Theme: standing on the poolside showing arm action with breathing	chin up as your pull back	all together	2 mins
walking through water, arm action with breathing	blow out into the water	all together	3 mins
dolphin kicks breathing every 4 kicks	breathe out slowly	waves	3 mins
push and glide adding kicks and breathing	1-2-3 breathe	waves	3 mins
full stroke breathing every stroke	inhale as your arms recover	waves	3 mins
full stroke breathing every other stroke	blow out hard as you lift your head	waves	3 mins
Contrasting Activity: tuck (mushroom) float	knees and chin to chest	all together	2 mins
pencil jump	jump away from the poolside	one by one	3 mins
Exit: using the pool steps or over the poolside	take your time	one by one	1 min

Total time: 27 minutes

Lesson #13 Assessment

Lesson Objective: to introduce basic butterfly breathing technique.		
Below average	**Average**	**Above average**
😐	🙂	😎
Attempts to demonstrate but does not show the correct technique	Able to perform most of the technique correctly some of the time	Performs the technique correctly most of the time

Assessment	😐	🙂	😎
Breathing is in time with the arm cycle			
Exhalation takes place in the water			
Inhalation takes place as the arms recover			

Lesson Plan #14

Lesson type: butterfly breathing
Level: adult or child intermediate
Previous learning: basic butterfly technique
Lesson aim: to develop breathing technique while performing the full stroke
Equipment: floats, buoyancy aids and hoop

Exercise/Activity	Teaching Points	Organisation	Duration
Entry: swivel entry	enter slowly	all together	1 min
Warm up: 2 widths any stroke	slow and gentle swim	all together	3 mins
Main Theme: 2 widths full stroke butterfly	continuous arms and legs	waves	3 mins
push and glide adding arm pulls, breathing every other pull	control your breath	waves	3 mins
dolphin kicks breathing every 2 kicks	kick, kick, breathe	waves	3 mins
dolphin kick with breaststroke arms, breathing every stroke	kick and blow	waves	3 mins
full stroke breathing every other stroke	blow out hard as you lift your head	waves	3 mins
full stroke breathing every stroke	inhale at the end of your arm pull	waves	3 mins
Contrasting Activity: push and glide through a submerged hoop	relax and stretch	2 or 3 at a time	3 mins
treading water for 60 seconds	mouth and nose out of the water	all together	2 mins
Exit: using the pool steps or over the poolside	take your time	one by one/all together	1 min

Total time: 28 minutes

Lesson #14 Assessment

Lesson Objective: to develop and progress basic butterfly breathing technique.		
Below average	**Average**	**Above average**
😐	🙂	😎
Attempts to demonstrate but does not show the correct technique	**Able to perform most of the technique correctly some of the time**	**Performs the technique correctly most of the time**

Assessment	😐	🙂	😎
Breathing is in time with the arm cycle			
Exhalation takes place in the water			
Inhalation takes place as the arms recover			
Breathing is continuous and unlabored*			

*allowances should be made for a swimmer's fitness and stamina levels, as these will affect breathing pattern and continuity.

Lesson Plan #15

Lesson type: butterfly breathing
Level: adult or child advanced
Previous learning: full stroke butterfly
Lesson aim: to develop and perfect butterfly breathing technique
Equipment: kickboard if needed and fins

Exercise/Activity	Teaching Points	Organisation	Duration
Entry: sitting or shallow dive entry	take your time	waves	1 min
Warm up: 2 lengths any stroke	take your time	all together	3 mins
Main Theme: 2 lengths full stroke butterfly	steady breathing	waves	2 mins
dolphin kicks using fins, breathing every 2 kicks	kick, kick, breathe	waves	3 mins
dolphin kick with breaststroke arms, breathing every other stroke	slow controlled breathing	waves	3 mins
full stroke with fins, breathing every other stroke	blow out hard as you lift your head	waves	3 mins
2 lengths full stroke - breathing every stroke	inhale at the end of your arm pull	waves	3 mins
2 lengths full stroke butterfly	continuous rhythmical breathing	waves	3 mins
Contrasting Activity: treading water - vary with 1 arm behind the back or above the water	ears and mouth above the surface	waves	3 mins
basic racing start	push hard from the legs	waves	3 mins
Exit: using the pool steps or over the poolside	take your time	one by one	1 min

Total time: 29 minutes

Lesson #15 Assessment

Lesson Objective: to develop and perfect butterfly breathing technique.	

Below average	Average	Above average
😐	🙂	😎
Attempts to demonstrate but does not show the correct technique	Able to perform most of the technique correctly some of the time	Performs the technique correctly most of the time

Assessment	😐	🙂	😎
Breathing is in time with the arm cycle			
Exhalation takes place in the water			
Inhalation takes place as the arms recover			
Breathing is 'explosive' when performed every stroke			

Lesson Plan #16

Lesson type: butterfly timing and coordination
Level: adult or child beginner
Previous learning: basic back paddle and butterfly arm movement
Lesson aim: to learn basic coordination of arms and legs for butterfly
Equipment: buoyancy aids and sinkers as necessary

Exercise/Activity	Teaching Points	Organisation	Duration
Entry: swivel entry	enter slowly	all together	1 min
Warm up: 2 widths any stroke using buoyancy aids	slow and gentle swim	all together	3 mins
Main Theme: 2 widths full stroke butterfly	arms and legs work together	waves	3 mins
push and glide adding leg kicks	count 2 kicks at a time	waves	3 mins
push and glide adding arm pulls	continuous arms	waves	3 mins
push and glide adding leg kicks and arm pulls - perform slowly at first	2 beat leg kick	waves	3 mins
1 width full stroke butterfly	kick head down, kick head up	waves	3 mins
2 widths full stroke butterfly	kick, pull, kick, recover	waves	3 mins
Contrasting Activity: prone star float	deep breath and relax	all together	2 mins
submerge to collect an object	eyes open	2 or 3 at a time	3 mins
Exit: using the pool steps or over the poolside	take your time	one by one	1 min

Total time: 28minutes

Lesson #16 Assessment

Lesson Objective: to introduce a basic butterfly timing pattern.		
Below average	**Average**	**Above average**
😐	🙂	😎
Attempts to demonstrate but does not show the correct technique	**Able to perform most of the technique correctly some of the time**	**Performs the technique correctly most of the time**

Assessment	😐	🙂	😎
Arms and legs are continuous			
2 beat leg kick			
Leg kicks are in time with the arm pull cycle			

Lesson Plan #17

Lesson type: butterfly timing and coordination
Level: adult or child intermediate
Previous learning: basic timing technique
Lesson aim: to progress and develop previous learning of butterfly timing
Equipment: buoyancy aids if needed and hoop

Exercise/Activity	Teaching Points	Organisation	Duration
Entry: swivel or sitting dive entry	enter slowly	waves/ all together	1 min
Warm up: 2 widths any stroke	take your time	all together	3 mins
Main Theme: 2 widths full stroke butterfly	arms and legs are continuous	all together	2 mins
push and glide adding leg kicks and arm pulls - perform slowly at first	2 beat leg kick	waves	3 mins
push and glide adding a single stroke cycle	kick the arms in and kick the arms out	waves	3 mins
leg kicks with breaststroke arms	kick, pull, kick, dive	waves	3 mins
1 width full stroke butterfly - perform slowly at first	kick, kick, throw the arms over	waves	3 mins
2 widths full stroke butterfly	kick, pull, kick, recover	waves	3 mins
Contrasting Activity: feet first surface dives through a submerged hoop	stretch up and sink	one by one	4 mins
feet first sculling	toes at the surface	waves	3 mins
Exit: using the pool steps	take your time	one by one	1 min

Total time: 29 minutes

Lesson #17 Assessment

Lesson Objective: to progress and develop previous learning of butterfly timing.		
Below average	**Average**	**Above average**
😐	🙂	😎
Attempts to demonstrate but does not show the correct technique	**Able to perform most of the technique correctly some of the time**	**Performs the technique correctly most of the time**

Assessment	😐	🙂	😎
Arms and legs are continuous			
2 beat leg kick			
'Kick, pull, kick, recover' sequence			
Timing is regular and rhythmical			

Lesson Plan #18

Lesson type: butterfly timing and coordination
Level: adult or child advanced
Previous learning: full stroke butterfly
Lesson aim: to develop and fine-tune butterfly timing
Equipment: floats and sinkers if needed, fins

Exercise/Activity	Teaching Points	Organisation	Duration
Entry: sitting or shallow dive entry	take your time	waves	1 min
Warm up: 2 lengths any stroke	take your time	all together	3 mins
Main Theme: 1 length full stroke butterfly	arms and legs are continuous	all together	2 mins
push and glide adding stroke cycles	2 beat leg kick	waves	3 mins
leg kicks with breaststroke arms	kick, pull, kick, dive	waves	3 mins
1 length full stroke butterfly - optional with fins	kick the arms in and kick the arms out	waves	3 mins
1 length full stroke butterfly counting stroke cycles	kick, kick, throw the arms over	waves	3 mins
2 lengths full stroke butterfly	kick, pull, kick, recover	waves	3 mins
Contrasting Activity: head first surface dive and swim underwater for a pre-set distance	deep breath and dig down deep	one by one	3 mins
basic racing start	fast transition to stroke	waves	3 mins
Exit: using the pool steps	take your time	one by one	1 min

Total time: 28 minutes

Lesson #18 Assessment

Lesson Objective: to develop and fine-tune butterfly timing.		
Below average	**Average**	**Above average**
😐	🙂	😎
Attempts to demonstrate but does not show the correct technique	Able to perform most of the technique correctly some of the time	Performs the technique correctly most of the time

Assessment	😐	🙂	😎
Arms and legs are continuous			
Kick occurs when the arms pull and then again as the arms recover			
'Kick, pull, kick, recover' sequence			
Timing is regular and rhythmical			

"Now that you have finished my book, would you please consider writing a review? Reviews are the best way readers discover great new books. I would truly appreciate it."

Mark Young

For more information about teaching swimming, learning to swim and improving swimming technique visit **Swim Teach**.

"The number one resource for learning to swim and improving swimming technique."

www.swim-teach.com

www.ingramcontent.com/pod-product-compliance
Lightning Source LLC
Chambersburg PA
CBHW062049090426
42740CB00016B/3068

* 9 7 8 0 9 9 5 4 8 4 2 5 2 *